Arthur Accused!

ISBN 979-11-91343-63-2 14740

Longtail Books

For my grandma Thora,

who would be so proud

Chapter 1

*Hello, stranger. I'm Buster Baxter, **private** eye. You can call me Buster for short. I'm going to tell you about my first **case**. It **involve**d my **pal** Arthur, some **missing quarter**s, and a whole lot of trouble.*

*The whole thing started two days ago. It was an **ordinary** Wednesday—the kind that comes right between Tuesday and Thursday. The middle of the week, when anything can happen—and usually does.*

The school day had just ended, and Arthur

was standing in the school **hallway** behind a long table. In front of him was a **bowl** half-filled with quarters.

"Help the **fire department** buy a new **puppy**!" Arthur called. "Only a quarter!"

A couple of kids dropped in quarters.

"Thanks," said Arthur. "Thanks a lot."

Binky Barnes walked up to him. His head and shoulders **block**ed the light from the **hall** window. "What's with the bowl, Arthur?"

"I'm **collect**ing money for Mrs. MacGrady's **fund drive**. We're going to buy a puppy for the fire department." He showed Binky a picture.

"That dog has a lot of **spot**s. You sure it isn't sick?"

"No, no. Dalmatians all look like that. So what do you think? How about a quarter?"

Binky **consider**ed it. He **weigh**ed the thought of a **shiny** quarter against a little

7

Dalmatian puppy. The puppy in his head **roll**ed over and made little **snuffling** sounds. It sat up and **wag**ged its tail. The quarter just sat there being shiny.

"Here," said Binky. He reached into his pocket and **flip**ped a quarter into the bowl. "There's just one thing," he added, **glaring** at Arthur.

"What's that?"

"Don't tell anybody I gave. It's bad for my image."

"Okay," said Arthur.

Binky seemed **satisfied**, at least for the moment.

"Hey, Arthur!" **yell**ed Buster as he ran down the hall.

"What's with the **goofy** hat?" asked Arthur.

"This hat is not goofy," said Buster. "It's a fedora*—part of my new **detective kit**. I've

---

★ **fedora** 페도라. 챙이 말려 있고 높이가 낮은 중절모.

8

been **snoop**ing—ah, looking for **crime**s."

"Have you found any?"

"No." Buster pushed back the **brim** of his hat. "But I did pick up some secret information."

He **peer**ed to the left and right, making sure no one else was listening.

"You promise this will **go no further**?"

Arthur **nod**ded.

Buster **lean**ed **forward**. "Third-grade picnic this Friday," he **whisper**ed.

Arthur **roll**ed **his eyes**. "I know that, Buster. There have been **sign**s up for two weeks."

"Oh. Well, I was half right. It's still information. Anyway, I'm not **giving up**. I'll find a crime. Maybe I'll find one at the **arcade**. My mom's taking me there this afternoon. Want to come?"

Most of the kids seemed to have gone

home. Arthur **figure**d he had **probably** collected all the quarters he was going to get for the day. And the arcade was a great place.

"Sure," he said. "Just let me take these quarters to Mrs. MacGrady."

He **emptied** the quarters from the bowl into a paper bag.

"I'll go find my mom outside," said Buster. "We'll wait for you. Hurry!"

Arthur nodded and ran down the hall.

Chapter 2

I wasn't with Arthur for the next few minutes. Maybe if I had been, he wouldn't have had any problems. But as it says in the **Detective**'s Handbook, *When life takes a wrong turn, just try not to get lost.*

Arthur hurried to the **cafeteria** kitchen. He could tell that Mr. Morris, the **janitor**, had cleaned the floors since lunch. "Clean enough to **eat off** of," Mr. Morris liked to say, but Arthur **prefer**red **plate**s.

Mrs. MacGrady **was on the phone**.

"What's that, **Chief**? Have you thought of a name yet?"

Arthur **wave**d, trying to get her **attention**. He didn't want to keep Buster and his mother waiting.

But Mrs. MacGrady didn't see him.

"Smokey. Sure, that's a nice name for a dog. I see, I see . . ."

Arthur tried to be **patient**. On the **counter** next to him were some **baking ingredient**s. There were bags of **flour** and sugar, **stick**s of butter, eggs, and chocolate **square**s.

"Where there's Smokey, there's a **firefighter**. Cute, Chief. Very cute. I just don't want the dog to get a **complex**. Dogs are **sensitive**, you know."

The bag was getting heavy in Arthur's hand. He went to put it down and **accidental**ly **knock**ed **over** the bag of flour.

"Chester's a fine name for a dog, don't you

think? My first husband was named Chester."

Since Mrs. MacGrady still wasn't watching, Arthur was able to clean up the flour without her seeing him. Some of it had gotten into the bag of **quarter**s, but that was okay because flour wouldn't do the quarters any **harm**.

Arthur looked at the clock. He had been standing there for more than five minutes.

"Mrs. MacGrady? Excuse me, Mrs. MacGrady?" He held up the bag of quarters.

She waved her hand, although whether she was waving to Arthur or making **motion**s to the phone, it was hard to know.

"I'm just leaving—," Arthur began.

But Mrs. MacGrady, still talking on the phone, had **turn**ed **away**.

Arthur couldn't wait any longer. If he did, Buster would have a **fit**. Mrs. MacGrady **was bound to** be off the phone soon.

"I'm leaving the bag on the counter,"

Arthur called out. "Right here, next to the flour."

Then he left.

Chapter 3

When Arthur and I arrived at the **arcade**, I had two things on my mind. One was the games themselves. I wanted a **return match** with **Alien Explore**r, which had **rough**ed me **up** the last time. That game needed to be **taught a lesson**. And I was just the one to do it.

The other thing on my mind was finding a mystery to **solve**. Arcades **draw shifty characters** the way a **garbage dump** draws flies. I **figure**d something would come my way if I kept a good **lookout**.

"Buster," said Arthur, "what are you doing with that **magnifying glass**?"

"Just checking things out." Buster was **peer**ing closely at a table. "Some mysteries like to play hide-and-seek.*" He moved the glass back to Arthur, looking up and down. "Look at you, for example."

"What *about* me?" said Arthur.

"You've got white **stuff** on your clothes."

"I do not."

Buster looked closer. "**Definite**ly some kind of powder."

Arthur looked down. There was a little . . . Suddenly he smiled. "Oh, that's no mystery. When I was dropping off the **quarter**s in the **cafeteria**, I **accidental**ly **spill**ed some **flour**. It must have gotten on my shirt."

Buster looked **disappoint**ed. "Well, it *could*

★ **hide-and-seek** 숨바꼭질.

17

have been a mystery."

"Sorry," said Arthur. "Anyway, I thought we were here to play."

They **made the rounds**, playing some games themselves and watching others play, too. Neither of them was very lucky at **surviving** *CrashCourse 2000* or **get**ting **through** the night at *Haunted Hotel*, but Buster did better at *Alien Explorer*.

"Take that, you **mangy mutant**!" he cried. "Ah, **revenge** is sweet!" The mutant had always **do**ne him **in** before.

"Just a few more minutes, boys," Buster's mother called out to them. She was waiting for them outside the arcade.

Buster was out of money, but Arthur still had enough for one more game. He decided to try a pinball machine. He put in his quarters and pulled the **knob**. As he **released** it, the ball **shot** up the **slot** and around the

ramp.

"Go, Arthur, go!" said Buster, who never had much luck at pinball.

The ball **ricochet**ed around the **platform**. Whenever it lost speed and fell **downward**, Arthur caught it with the **flip**per⋆ and sent it up again.

"Whoa! That was close, Arthur! **Keep it up**."

As Arthur's score rose, the machine **lit** up in more and more colors. A crowd began to gather behind him.

"**Watch out**, there!"

"Hold it . . . now!"

Arthur was **on a roll**.

"Go for the spinner!⋇"

Arthur did his best, but finally the third

⋆ **flipper** 핀볼 게임 기계에서 위에서 내려오는 공을 받아 쳐올리는 장치.
⋇ **spinner** 스피너. 핀볼 게임 기계 속 기둥 모양의 장치로, 회전하면서 공이 닿으면 사방으로 튕겨내는 역할을 한다.

20

ball **dodge**d the right flipper and **sank** into the hole.

"Arthur, you did it!" cried Buster. "You hit the high score!"

Arthur looked up. His 868,233 points were in first place. He even got to put his **initial**s next to them.

"That score will stand forever," said Buster. He **pound**ed Arthur on the back as the **onlooker**s **cheer**ed.

When they left the arcade, Buster was still excited. "My best friend hit the high score," he said **proud**ly to **one and all**.

It wasn't the same as finding a mystery to solve, but it was still pretty good.

Chapter 4

As much as I hated to **admit** it, I was starting to feel a little down. Why was it so hard to find a mystery to **investigate**? Did all **detectives** have these problems? Still, at least I had some good news to share at school the next day.

"Step **aside**, everyone. Make way! Pinball **wizard** coming through."

Buster made these **comment**s as he and Arthur walked down the **hall**.

"Buster, please!" said Arthur. "It's **embarrass**ing."

"Don't be so **modest**, Arthur. You **deserve** the **attention**."

Arthur **sigh**ed.

"**Nimble** fingers here! Eyes like a **hawk**. **Reflex**es like a cat!"

As they passed the **principal**'s office, Mr. Haney **wave**d them in.

"Good morning, Arthur, Buster," he said. "Oh, Arthur, don't forget to give Mrs. MacGrady the **quarter**s you **collect**ed for her **fund drive**."

"I already did, Mr. Haney."

The school **secretary**, Miss Tingley, **frown**ed. "That's **odd**. She told me she never got them."

"Aha!" said Buster. "Maybe they were **stolen**."

"Buster, please **contain** yourself," said Mr. Haney. The principal turned to Arthur. "Is it possible you brought them home by mistake?"

"No," said Buster. "He came straight to the **arcade** with me. In fact, he did very well at pinball. You're looking at Mr. High Score."

"Really?" Mr. Haney frowned. Miss Tingley frowned, too.

"I got the high score once," Buster **went on**. "**Cost** me a **fortune**. Took all my birthday money. Like a hundred quarters. Boy,★ did I—"

Buster stopped suddenly. He **stare**d at Arthur. So did Mr. Haney and Miss Tingley.

"What's the matter?" asked Arthur.

"We have a little mystery here," said Mr. Haney.

Miss Tingley frowned again. "Not so little," she said.

A short while later, Arthur found himself sitting in the principal's office. He felt very small. The chair he was sitting in was very uncomfortable.

★ **boy** 어머나, 맙소사. 일반적으로 알고 있는 '소년'이라는 의미가 아니라, 놀라움과 안타까움을 나타내는 감탄사로 쓰였다.

"You were **responsible** for the money," Mr. Haney was saying.

"You **certain**ly were," Miss Tingley added.

Arthur **shrank farther** into the chair.

He looked from one **stern** face to the other. "You mean . . . you think *I* stole the quarters? But I left them on the **cafeteria counter**."

"Well, Mrs. MacGrady never saw them," Mr. Haney said. "You were responsible for them. If that money doesn't **turn up**, I'm afraid you'll have to **serve** a day—"

Miss Tingley cleared her **throat**.

"I mean, a week of after-school **detention**." Mr. Haney **pause**d. "And no third grade picnic for you tomorrow."

Arthur was **horrified**.

As he left the office, Buster **rush**ed up to him.

"So what happened?"

Arthur explained it to him. "My first

important job, and everyone thinks I'm a **thief**. But I'm **innocent**."

"Of course you are," said Buster. "That's why you need a detective. Like, say . . . me."

"I don't know, Buster. Do you really think you can find out what happened to the quarters?"

"No problem! I could **solve** this **case** in my sleep. Well, no, I guess I'd have to be **awake**. And not wearing my **pajamas**, either. But don't worry, Arthur. Buster Baxter is on the case. You'll be going to that picnic tomorrow. **Trust** me."

Arthur wanted to believe him, but he wished he felt more hopeful. "Okay, Buster, do your **stuff**. But promise me one thing."

"Sure. What is it?"

"Try not to get me into any deeper trouble than I'm in now. Things are bad enough **as it is**."

Chapter 5

*In every **case** there's a **key witness**, and this case was no different. I knew who she was, and* she *knew who she was, too.*

Last name: MacGrady.

First name: Mrs.

***Occupation**: **Cafeteria** lady.*

Buster found Mrs. MacGrady in the cafeteria kitchen. She was mixing **ingredient**s in a large **bowl**. He explained that he was **investigating** the **disappearance** of Arthur's **quarter**s.

"Can you tell me your **whereabouts** yesterday afternoon?" he asked.

"'Whereabouts,' huh? That's a pretty **fancy** way of asking me where I was. Well, I was right here in the kitchen, making brownies. Buster, keep your hands away from that bowl!"

"Aha!" said Buster, pulling back his hand. "Maybe I should **taste** this. It could be **evidence**."

Mrs. MacGrady **wave**d a **spatula** at him. "Nice try. But you'll have to wait for the picnic like everyone else."

She moved over to a long table covered with tiny cherry tarts★ and began **squirt**ing **whip**ped cream onto each one.

"I remember speaking to the **chief**. We had quite a long conversation. Then I made the

---

★ **tart** 타르트. 반죽 위에 과일이나 크림 같이 달콤한 것을 가득 올리고 구워 만든 파이.

brownies."

"Did you see Arthur?"

"No, I didn't see anyone all afternoon. Oh, wait, that's not true. Mr. Morris was here. My mixer **jam**med a few times, and the brownie mix **overflow**ed onto the floor. He came in to **mop** up the **mess**."

"Hmmm," said Buster, **pop**ping one of the cherry tarts into his mouth.

"Maybe you should talk to Mr. Morris," Mrs. MacGrady **suggest**ed.

"Mank you fery huch,*" Buster **mumble**d, and ran out before she could say anything.

He found Mr. Morris, the school **janitor**, pushing a cart along the **hallway**.

"Excuse me, Mr. Morris," said Buster. "May I ask you a couple of questions?"

"Shoot."

★ **Mank you fery huch** 'thank you very much'를 음식을 몰래 먹으면서 말하느라 발음이 분명치 않다.

Buster explained that he was trying to re-create the **sequence** of events from the **previous** afternoon.

"'Sequence of events,' eh?" said Mr. Morris. "You sound like one of those TV **detective** shows."

"Really?" said Buster. He **beam**ed. Then he remembered that detectives don't beam and tried to look **serious** again.

"Tell me about yesterday."

"Well, let's see," said Mr. Morris. "I was in the teachers' room—"

"Aha!" said Buster **suspicious**ly. "And *what* were you doing there?"

"Changing a **lightbulb**. Then I got the call to go to the kitchen. Seems Mrs. MacGrady was having some trouble with her mixer. When I got there, the floor was covered with brownie **batter**. So I cleaned up the mess."

Buster **fold**ed his arms. "And do you *always*

clean up after Mrs. MacGrady?"

"No, not often. She's pretty **tidy as a rule**. But I was glad to help. Anything else?"

Buster wanted to think of more questions. He liked asking questions. But he couldn't think of any.

"Not at the moment. But do me a **favor** and don't leave town."

Mr. Morris smiled. "**Whatever you say**, Buster."

He gathered up his **bucket** and mop and started to walk away. With each step he made a **jingling** sound.

"Just a minute, Mr. Morris." Buster ran to **catch up** to him. "That jingling . . . It sounds like quarters. *A lot of quarters!*"

Mr. Morris pulled a **huge** key ring full of keys from his pocket. "I know what you mean," he said, jingling it. "I've often thought the same thing myself."

"Oh. Well, that's all right, then."

It wasn't really all right, thought Buster, at least not for Arthur. He had hoped to **get to the bottom of** the case quickly. But the more he **dug**, the more **complicated** the case became.

And the bottom was nowhere in **sight**.

Chapter 6

*I had been on the job a couple of hours, but **aside** from one cherry tart, I had little to show for it. Nobody was calling the **suspect** a **liar**, but nobody could **support** his story, either. I thought maybe a change of **scene** would help, so I made my way to the suspect's home. There I met up with the suspect's sister. She seemed to be a pretty **cool customer** but I knew I could **handle** her.*

"Come on, D.W., you must know *something*."

They were standing in the Reads' kitchen. Arthur had gone out for a while, D.W. had said. But he couldn't go far, she **figured**. The police were **probably** watching the train and bus stations. "And his pictures are probably on Wanted posters★ by now," she said.

"D.W., I'm trying to **clear** Arthur, not send him to **jail**. Now think hard."

D.W. **made a face**. "All right, all right, I'll tell you what I know."

"**Go on**." Buster got out his **pad** and pencil.

"Ready? Okay, **take** this **down**. Every single word."

Buster **nod**ded.

"THAT . . . HAT . . . LOOKS . . . **SILLY** . . . ON . . . YOU."

Buster put down his pencil. "This is **serious**, D.W. **Besides**, I like the hat."

D.W. **giggle**d.

"Now back to the **subject** at—"

★ **wanted poster** 지명 수배 광고.

"What is this, Buster, the **third degree**? If I knew anything, I'd **certain**ly tell . . . well, maybe not you. But somebody."

Buster pushed back his fedora. "Don't try that **smoke screen stuff** on me. I can see through you like a window. Now, think back to yesterday. Did Arthur bring home any big **jingling** bags . . . you know, **absentminded**ly?"

D.W. **glare**d at him. "Buster, you're talking about my brother! He would never take other people's money and bring it home like that."

"Calm down, D.W. I don't think Arthur would do anything bad **on purpose**. But he could have been **forgetful**. I'm just checking out every **possibility**."

"Arthur's **not that** stupid," D.W. went on. Clearly, she had been giving the matter some serious thought. "He wouldn't just bring the money into the house. Too many questions to answer. Too many people might see it. But he'd want it **close by**. Hidden. Safe. But where? That's what I can't quite **figure out**. Not that Arthur's so **clever**. But still . . ."

She **scratch**ed her head.

"Of course!" she shouted. "We should check the **lawn** for **sign**s of **recent dig**ging."

"But D.W.—"

She ran out the door. But before Buster could follow her, Arthur walked in.

"Oh, Buster! I'm glad you're here. Does this mean good news?"

"Sorry, Arthur. The **case** is still wide open."

Arthur **sigh**ed.

"I'm just trying to be **thorough**," Buster explained. "**Detective**s need to be thorough."

"Buster, if you don't find out who did it by tomorrow, I'll **miss** the picnic."

"I know. I haven't—"

He **hesitate**d as D.W. passed by, carrying a

shovel.

"Excuse me. Step aside. Coming through."

Arthur **stare**d at D.W. and started to say something, but Buster held up his hand.

"You**'re better off** not asking," he said. "You really don't want to know."

Chapter 7

*The situation did not look good. Everything still pointed to just one person—Arthur. Could he really be a **criminal mastermind**? I tried to **picture** him in his secret **hideout**, swimming in a sea of **shiny quarters**. They **dripp**ed through his fingers as he laughed **insanely**. Quarters! Quarters! He could never get enough.*

Dinner at the Baxter house was quiet that evening. Mrs. Baxter **was used to** hear**ing** Buster talk all about his day. But tonight Buster was quiet. Too quiet.

"Are you feeling all right?" his mother asked.

Buster **nod**ded.

"But you've only had two **helping**s of **dessert**. That's not like you, Buster. You're sure you don't have a **headache** or **fever**?"

Buster shook his head. "It's just this **case**, Mom. I haven't **figure**d **out** how to help Arthur yet."

"You're a good friend, Buster. I'm sure Arthur **appreciate**s that."

"I hope so." But right now, thought Buster, Arthur needs more than a good friend. He needs a good **detective**.

Later, Buster sat at his desk, **flip**ping through his **pad**. He was looking for **clue**s, any clues that would help him **solve** the case. He wasn't feeling **picky**, either. Big clues, small clues, **ragged**-round-the-edges clues— Buster would have happily **accept**ed *any* of them.

The phone rang.

"Buster, it's for you."

It was the Brain. He **wonder**ed if Buster was having any luck.

"Not yet," Buster **report**ed.

"Well, keep trying. If I think of anything, I'll call you back."

A few minutes later, the phone rang again. This time it was Francine.

"Any **progress**?" she asked.

"No," said Buster.

"Okay. Keep me **inform**ed."

He had **barely** put down the phone when it rang again. Now Muffy was on the line. "It's too bad we can't buy clues," she said. "That would make things so much easier."

Buster **agree**d. But clues just weren't **for sale**.

After that the phone was quiet. Buster

lay on his bed as a **swirl** of images—Mrs. MacGrady, Mr. Morris, and Arthur—passed by in his mind. They were all **involve**d **somehow**. He just had to put the pieces of the puzzle together.

"Buster, it's getting late!"

"I'm trying to **crack** the case."

"Well, you need your sleep, Mr. Detective. You're not a robot."

"You're right, I'm not a . . ." Buster **leap**t to his feet. "Robot! That's it! Mom, I love you!"

He went to the phone and **dial**ed Arthur.

"Hello?" said Arthur.

"Great news!" shouted Buster. "I figured it out!"

"Really?" Arthur got all excited. "So, tell me."

"Okay. Well, the quarters were **stolen** by an **army** of **evil** robots. They need the metal for **fuel**. Nobody **notice**d them because they can

transform themselves into . . . into . . . any **shape**."

Arthur **sigh**ed. "That's it? That's your big **breakthrough**?"

"Gosh, it sounded a lot better a minute ago. . . ."

"You'd better get some sleep," said Arthur.

"Okay," said Buster. "You too."

"I'll try," said Arthur. But if his only chance **depend**ed on finding an army of robots, he figured he **was in for** a long night.

Chapter
8

Detectives are supposed to be tough, but even they feel the pain when a friend is hurting. And it was no different for me. I could tell from Arthur's eyes that he was not happy. Actually, I could tell from his mouth, the slump of his shoulders, even his ears. Arthur was a mess.

"Are you sure you want to be seen with me?" Arthur asked on the way to school the next morning.

"Of course," said Buster.

"People might begin to think you're

my partner in **crime**. You could be my **accomplice**, my **henchman**, my—"

"Arthur, stop! Listen, I would never **desert** you. I'm no **rat** leaving a **sink**ing ship. Why,★ even if you went to **jail**, I would write you. I would come visit. Well, you know . . ."

Buster **realize**d this wasn't helping much. "Anyway," he added, "I'm really sorry you're going to **miss** the picnic today. And it's because I'm a bad detective. I know you're **innocent**."

Arthur tried to smile. "Thanks, Buster."

"I hate **let**ting you **down**. If I just had a little more time."

"Forget it," said Arthur. "You did your best. You might be a **lousy** detective—"

"*Bad*, Arthur. I said *bad*."

"Oh, right. You might be a bad detective,

★**why** 오, 아니, 이런, 어머. 이유를 묻는 '왜'라는 의문사가 아니라, 놀라거나 의외라는 반응을 나타내는 감탄사로 쓰였다.

48

but you're still a good friend."

Buster and Arthur soon arrived at school. Buster got in line for the picnic bus with the other kids.

Mr. Ratburn **motion**ed to Arthur.

"Sorry about this, Arthur."

"Me, too, Mr. Ratburn."

His teacher **nod**ded. "Don't **give up**. I'm sure the truth will come out in the end."

Arthur **certain**ly hoped so.

"Children!" Mr. Haney shouted through his **bullhorn**. "Please **board** the school bus now."

Buster was standing with Binky and the Brain. They started to move **forward**.

"Poor Arthur," said the Brain.

"A good **lawyer** could **get** him **off**," said Binky. "They do it all the time."

"But Arthur's innocent," said Buster. "I just don't know how to **prove** it. The answer's

somewhere right in front of me. Hey, what's that?"

He pointed to Binky's shirt.

Binky looked down. "Powdered sugar, I guess. I had a doughnut on the way to school."

"Oh. See, that's a **clue**. If this was the **case** of the **missing** doughnuts, I'd **be all set**." Buster **frown**ed. "I just can't think straight anymore."

"I know how you feel," said the Brain. "Sometimes when I'm working on a tough math problem, I feel like my brain's **overflow**ing with data."

"Keep it moving," said Mr. Haney.

Buster stepped onto the bus. Suddenly he stopped and **stare**d at the Brain.

"Overflowing? Overflowing!"

"I think the **pressure got to him**," Binky **whisper**ed.

"That's it!" cried Buster. He shook the Brain's hand. "That's it!"

"What's it?" said the Brain.

Buster **race**d off the bus and almost ran into Mr. Haney.

"**Hold on** there, Buster. You're going the wrong way."

"Mr. Haney! I've **solve**d the crime. Come on!"

Without waiting for an answer, he led the way into the school.

Chapter 9

*Every **detective** wants to be cool, calm, and **collected at all times**. And I was no different. But it's easy to say that while you're **sitting back** in your office with your feet up on the desk. It's another thing when you think you've saved your best friend from a **fate** worse than death.*

In the kitchen, Mrs. MacGrady was **pack**ing up for the school picnic. She had the sandwiches, potato chips, and **carton**s of juice all **neatly organize**d on the **counter**.

She was just getting ready to cut the **sheet**

of brownies into **square**s when Buster **rush**ed in. He was pulling Mr. Haney behind him. "Slow down, Buster," said Mr. Haney. "We don't want to be **arrest**ed for **speeding**."

Mrs. MacGrady looked **surprise**d. "Buster! Mr. Haney! What are you doing here?"

Mr. Haney cleared his **throat**. "**Follow**ing **up on** a **theory**. Go ahead, Buster."

"Mrs. MacGrady, do you know why your brownie mix **overflow**ed?"

"Not really. I don't mind saying it was a little **embarrass**ing. But Mr. Morris was very nice about helping me clean it up."

"Has that ever happened before? The overflowing, I mean."

"No. I'm always very careful. But this time I guess I made too much."

"Did you use a different **recipe**?"

Mrs. MacGrady stopped to think. "Well, no, **now that** you **mention** it. The recipe was the same as always."

"Did you use any new **equipment**?"

Mrs. MacGrady laughed. "Not on my **budget**. I'm lucky they give me **electricity**."

Mr. Haney cleared his throat.

Buster picked up a knife and cut a square out of the brownie pan.

"And yet **somehow** something happened, something that had never happened before. **Significant**, don't you think?"

Mr. Haney **fold**ed his arms. "Buster, **make your point**, please. The bus is waiting."

Buster was getting to it. But detectives never rush their moments of **glory**.

"So you **measure**d out the **ingredient**s in the usual way. And you mixed them in the usual way. And yet something unusual happened. Shall I tell you why?"

Mrs. MacGrady smiled. "Please do."

"It's because you **accidental**ly **include**d one

extra ingredient."

"I did?"

Buster **nod**ded. He picked up the brownie and broke it in two.

A **quarter** fell out.

"Oh, my," said Mrs. MacGrady. "How did that happen?"

"It was Arthur," Buster explained. "You were on the phone when he came in. He thought you saw him, but you didn't. Then he left the bag of quarters next to the other ingredients. He had even **spill**ed some of your **flour** on his bag, which is **probably** why you didn't **notice**."

Mrs. MacGrady broke open another brownie, and two quarters fell out.

"So now we know the truth," said Mr. Haney.

"Arthur is **innocent**!" Buster **exclaim**ed. "It's time to **set** him **free**."

Chapter

10

One kind of **detective fades** back into the **shadows** once a **case** is **solved**. For that detective, solving the mystery is its own **reward**. He **dodges** the bright lights of the television cameras and the front page of the newspaper.

The other kind of detective likes to take a **bow**, to be **recognized** for doing good work. He doesn't **duck** the well-**deserved compliment**. I could see both sides, and I understood that some detectives would be shy about taking **credit** for **untangling** things.

But I wasn't one of them.

Arthur was sitting in **detention** alone with his thoughts. And at that **particular** moment, his thoughts were not very good **company**. The **quarter**s were gone, and his **reputation** was **in question**. Even if he was someday **prove**d **innocent**, he was still going to **miss** the third-grade picnic.

He could hear Miss Tingley **typing** in the next room. The clicking on the keyboard made Arthur think of **cricket**s **chirp**ing. At least crickets were free to do what they wanted. They didn't have to worry about quarters or picnics or **unexpected** mysteries.

Suddenly Arthur heard another noise. This didn't sound like crickets at all. It sounded like *a lot* of people on the move.

Miss Tingley heard it, too. She stopped typing and got up to see what all the **commotion** was about.

It *was* a lot of people. The whole third grade was coming down the **hall**. The students, the teachers, and even the bus driver were there.

"What's going on?" Miss Tingley asked.

"Stand back," Mr. Haney **advise**d her. He opened the door to the room where Arthur was sitting. "**Justice** is about to be **serve**d."

"Arthur, I did it!" shouted Buster. "You're free."

Arthur stood up.

"I am? But how?"

"We've solved the mystery of the **missing** quarters," Mr. Haney explained. "They **end**ed **up** in Mrs. MacGrady's brownies."

"Really?" said Arthur. He looked at Mr. Ratburn, who smiled at him.

"They must be the richest brownies she's ever made," said the Brain.

Everyone laughed.

"And," said Buster, "you **owe** it all to that

great detective, that **peerless investigator**—"

Buster was cut off as Mr. Haney spoke into the **bullhorn.**

"Back to the bus, everyone!" he **order**ed. "The picnic **await**s."

As the kids went back outside, Arthur shook Buster's hand.

"Thanks, Buster. I'm almost **speechless.** You're the best detective I know!"

"I'm the *only* detective you know."

"Well, yes, but you're still the best."

"If you say so."

"I do."

"All right."

*He **went on** like that all the way out to the bus. I didn't try to stop him. A good detective knows when to sit back and listen.*

*The picnic was a big success. Later, though, Mrs. MacGrady faced a new mystery when a **plate** of*

cookies she had put **aside** suddenly disappeared.

I **brush**ed a few **crumb**s off my shirt and joined in the baseball game that was starting up. If Mrs. MacGrady wanted to solve that mystery, she was going to have to do it **on her own**.